Unstoppable

Seven Universal Laws That Will Transform How You Pursue and Achieve Success

Ralph Graves Jr.

Copyright © 2019 by **Ralph Graves Jr.**

All rights reserved. No part of this publication may be reproduced, distributed, or transmitted in any form or by any means, without prior written permission.

Scripture quotations marked (ESV) are taken from The ESV® Bible (The Holy Bible, English Standard Version®) copyright © 2001 by Crossway, a publishing ministry of Good News Publishers. ESV® Text Edition: 2011. The ESV® text has been reproduced in cooperation with and by permission of Good News Publishers. Unauthorized reproduction of this publication is prohibited. Used by permission. All rights reserved.

Scripture quotations marked (GNT) are taken from the Good News Translation in Today's English Version (Second Edition). Copyright © 1992 by American Bible Society. Used by permission.

Scripture quotations marked (NASB) are taken from the New American Standard Bible ® (NASB), copyright © 1960, 1962, 1963, 1968, 1971, 1972, 1973, 1975, 1977, 1995 by The Lockman Foundation. Used by permission. www.Lockman.org.

Speak It To Book
www.speakittobook.com

Unstoppable / Ralph Graves Jr.
ISBN-13: 978-1-945793-76-9
ISBN-10: 1-945793-76-7

To the memory of Shirley A. Prunty, my beloved mother-in-law. Thank you for showing us the way.

CONTENTS

Tried and True 3
The Law of Control 9
The Law of Intelligent Practice 19
The Law of Mental Equivalency 31
The Law of Expectation 41
The Law of Reciprocity 51
The Law of Habit 63
The Law of Forgiveness 73
Life According to the Laws 85
Notes 91
Recommended Reading 95
About the Author 97
About Speak It To Book 99

INTRODUCTION

Tried and True

This is not where anybody expected I would end up.

Founder and pastor of a church? Married to the same woman for twenty-seven years? Retired police sergeant? Founder of a community development organization? Motivational speaker?

Not likely, if you'd known me in my growing-up years. I was raised in a loving Christian home with two godly parents, but otherwise, I had few of the advantages—either materially or temperamentally—you would think necessary for a successful life.

I was strong-willed, which is to say that I was plain old hard-headed. I was full of head knowledge from church but had little capacity to apply godly wisdom to my life. I failed seventh grade. I ran with the crowd that was always in some kind of trouble. I got my high school girlfriend pregnant. I dropped out of college and football, didn't make the cut in the U.S. Coast Guard, and worked blue-collar jobs.

Yet here I am, by the grace of God, successful when no

one really thought I would be. I have become someone who sets and meets goals—thriving in life and reaching my potential while honoring God through my words and actions.

Wherever you are right now, this can be your trajectory, too. That's why I wrote this book: to help you know how to succeed in life, whether or not you have the advantages you think you need in terms of resources or personality.

The secret is following the laws—the universal laws in this book, that is. Over more than two decades, I have learned many principles of leadership and success from leaders in the field, such as John Maxwell, Zig Ziglar, and Les Brown. Through their teaching, my own experience, and biblical principles, I've come to believe there are seven key principles that can change the way we pursue and achieve happiness and success. These principles are laws proven to help people reach their full potential.

The seven principles of successful living we will explore in this book are:

- the Law of Control
- the Law of Intelligent Practice
- the Law of Mental Equivalency
- the Law of Expectation
- the Law of Reciprocity
- the Law of Habit
- the Law of Forgiveness

I will elaborate on these laws in detail, explaining how each is grounded in practical and biblical wisdom—and how applying it can transform your life.

But first, let me tell you my story so you'll better understand how these seven laws have already been tried and found true.

My Story

I was born in the late 1960s, to a father who worked in government and pastored a church and a mother who was an educator. It was a loving, stable home, and economically, I grew up solidly middle-class.

I saw the adults around me punching the clock for twenty or thirty years for the steady assurance of a good job, but I knew from an early age it wasn't what I wanted. I wanted to take risks, try, fail, and try again—to do something completely different.

My brother and I went to church every Sunday, and I was taught always to do the right thing. I daydreamed my way through my Christian grade school and public high school—a solid C and D student who had to repeat seventh grade. I did just enough to get by while I spent most of my time looking out the window. My friends and I got into all the trouble we could, short of gang membership.

A year after graduating high school, I was in college, playing football, and suddenly learned my girlfriend—an A student still in high school—was pregnant. It was a classic case of a high school princess and a bad boy. She almost didn't get to participate in the graduation ceremony because of the school's official policy against pregnant teens at the event. Three decades later, I'm still pained to think of the shame I caused her.

So I dropped football, dropped college, and joined the U.S. Coast Guard. Even though we weren't married, every paycheck was sent to Tina to take care of her and our daughter, Jazmin. I worked hard in the Coast Guard, but after a stint in which I got so seasick that I lost sixteen pounds, the Guard insisted on giving me a medical honorable discharge. I went through three more jobs—collecting trash, working in a factory for the railroad company, and working as a security guard—before I joined the police force. I've now retired after two decades on the force.

It was when I became a security guard, earning $18,000 per year, that I finally asked Tina to marry me. I had always had a job but never stayed at one for a long time. So, what did other people tell her? "He doesn't stick with anything—don't marry him."

But she said to them, "There's something in him no one can see but me." To this day, I am grateful beyond measure for her taking that chance on me.

As a Christian, I personally believe God opens doors for you: someone unexpectedly believes in you, advocates for you, gives you a chance, or provides for a specific opportunity to come to fruition. And I believe God guides you.

I grabbed a John Maxwell book one day while sitting in a police car, and it wasn't long before I'd devoured everything he had written—along with Zig Ziglar, Jim Rohn, Tony Robbins, and other gurus. As I began to apply the principles they taught, I noticed that independently of one another, these men had communicated advice based on the seven laws I'm going to share with you. Those laws are found in the Bible, but they work for everyone.

I know what it feels like to work hard. I know what it feels like to think of yourself as inadequate. I know what it means to cry at night—to want to fly away from it all. I know what it means to work outside of the system of these universal laws, stumbling and wandering. And I know the freedom and empowerment that comes from following them.

In This Book

I have devoted one chapter to each of the seven laws. We will discuss the importance of:

- self-control
- working smarter instead of simply working harder
- being aware how much our thoughts shape us
- having an attitude of confidence
- serving others
- creating good habits
- showing forgiveness to those who wrong us

Each chapter will explain one of the seven laws, present examples of how it works in real life, and offer you some practical advice for personal application of the law. At the end of each chapter, a workbook section will help you reflect intentionally on how the law is relevant to your life.

Ultimately, you need to follow every law if you expect successful results. However, don't try to start following all of them at once. Incorporate them one at a time until you work your way up to applying all seven laws consistently in your life. Taking small, sustainable steps is far superior to taking on too much initially, becoming overwhelmed, and dismissing the entire program as a result.

It is essential that you gather others around you who will help you. Drop the naysayers and surround yourself with those who will believe in you, encourage you, and challenge you as you put these principles into practice. If you have the right accountability partners, your journey will be much easier and far more likely to succeed.

It's time to decide that the transformation of your life begins *now*.

CHAPTER ONE

The Law of Control

In my early married years, I lived by the half-joking motto "Happy Wife, Happy Life." I worried chiefly about pleasing my wife and children: Were they happy? Fulfilled? Did my wife have time for her own pursuits? Was I always available to my children? There was no time for me to go to the gym, to take up a hobby, to take care of my own soul.

Or at least, I *thought* those things were unaffordable luxuries. I was beholden to external control over my life—to those I loved most, sure, but still beholden. And frankly, it wasn't healthy for *any* of us.

Similarly, in twenty years as a police officer, I was subject to a lot of external controls on my life: what days I was working, when my shift started and ended, who I was working with, what my beat was, which days I could request off (much less *get*). Even as I got fifteen, sixteen, and seventeen years on the police force under my belt, I accrued little external control.

Contrast that to a decision I made not long ago: to hire a driver. I realized I was wasting so much time in the car—forty-five minutes here, forty-five minutes there, multiple times a week. By hiring a driver, I gained control over those hours and could use my time in the car to answer emails and phone calls. I could bless a small business owner (the driver) with my business and use my time in the office more productively.

Is hiring a driver a luxury? Many might think so, but not in this case. In this case, it grants me more control, not for its own sake, but for the sake of accomplishing my goals more efficiently.

We all have some external controls over our lives. Few of us get to control everything about our schedules (even the self-employed are accountable for their work time), relationships (you don't get to choose your family), or finances (paying taxes isn't optional). But that doesn't mean we're victims of our circumstances. It doesn't mean we come home, veg in front of Netflix, and wake up twenty years from now wondering why we feel so unfulfilled.

If you want to be successful, the first law to follow is the *Law of Control*. Everyone can exercise internal control, and to varying extents, everyone can exercise external control, too.

The Law of Control has a lot to do with whether you feel positive or negative about yourself. We must spend time becoming who we are designed to be, whether or not that conforms to the person others expect or ask us to be. According to Brian Tracy, the Law of Control says this: "You feel good about yourself to the degree to which you feel that you are in control of your own life."[1] In other words, you must fully control your outlook on your life, and as much as you can of the externals in your life, so they are in harmony with your goals. You must take responsibility for your actions and control your time management, relationships, and major decisions.

The idea of taking control of our lives, insofar as possible, is certainly a biblical one. According to 2 Timothy 1:7, "God gave us a spirit not of fear but of power and love and self-control" (ESV). In 1 Corinthians 6:12, Paul wrote, "'All things are lawful for me,' but not all things are helpful. 'All things are lawful for me,' but I will not be dominated by anything" (ESV). The Bible teaches us to walk a narrow path—saying no to sinful desires that try to control us and lead to bad consequences and, instead, choosing the way that leads to a full, spiritually healthy life.

Clearly, we must control how and what we think—it is the beginning of maximizing our lives. When we take charge of controlling our internal landscape, it will naturally affect our external circumstances. We will have a clearer focus that allows us to take or leave the options with which we are presented every day. It takes us out of "living by accident," as Brian Tracy says.[2]

A victim mentality, even if you *have* been a victim, will never serve you well. Do what you must to extricate yourself from any and all situations that truly keep you down or hold you back, but don't get stuck into thinking that circumstances or others control you.

Don't just careen from one thing to another with no focus. Be intentional. You don't want to get to the end of your day and wonder where the day went—how another day passed without you taking control and taking care of yourself. You are not required to be available 24/7, though some people in your life won't like that.

Be intentional. Control what you eat. Control how you see the world. Say no to the things and people who are negative. As much as you are able, control your own schedule. (Hire a driver, if you need to!) Don't merely go through the motions of letting life *happen to* you.

The tools for realizing your destiny are *inside* of you. You control your outlook. You control how you prioritize your time. You control how you will handle your business, your family, and your various responsibilities. You are calling the shots. And so, even when you take a risk and it fails (which will happen), you still succeeded, because *you* were the one who called the shot and took the risk. You will learn from your failure because it belongs to you alone.

Sometimes we have to learn the valuable twin skills of eliminating and delegating. On eliminating: Will everything get done? Maybe, maybe not. The real question, if you are following the Law of Control, is: "Do all the tasks on this list *need* to be done? Do they fit within my goals?" If the answer is no, eliminate that task. Warren Buffet says, "The difference between successful people and really successful people is that really successful people say no to almost everything."[3]

On delegating: Will others do the task as well as you? Or the precise way you want it done? Maybe, maybe not. When following the Law of Control ask, "Are you really the only one who can do this task?" If the answer is no, delegate that task. One benefit is that you gain more control over your time; another is that someone else has the chance to carry out the task. And who knows? They may do it better than you, or they may learn something new in the implementation.

It's important to note that the Law of Control is *not* about controlling other people or gaining "the upper hand" over others. The Law of Control *is* about your *own* control over your *own* actions and decisions. It is about taking responsibility for becoming who you are designed to be.

Now, Apply This

Begin to live intentionally. Think about why you're doing what you're doing and make decisions based on what will help you achieve your goals.

To begin, choose an area of your life in which you are on autopilot. Is it your eating habits? Your exercise routine (or lack thereof)? Your weekly or daily schedule? Your finances? Who you spend time with, and what you do together?

When you've decided on an area of focus—choose only one at a time—write down what that area of your life would look like if you were to be intentional about it. Be specific.

For example, if you're currently on autopilot regarding your finances, write down a plan to be in control of your money. Financial planning expert Dave Ramsey says, "Stop wondering where your money goes every month, and start telling it where to go instead."[4] If that's not a clear statement of exercising control, I don't know what is!

Once you have a plan in place—and it's crucial that you write it down, along with the steps for achieving it—get to work on it. If it's finances, make a realistic budget and begin implementing it immediately. If it's relationships, make a list of those who pour into your life positively, or those to whom you're called as a giver (mentor, parent, etc.). Meanwhile, kindly but firmly begin to eliminate those who would be negative toward you or controlling of you.

Do you want to succeed in your goals? Then you must take control in every way you can.

This will take practice. But it must be *intelligent* practice—which is the next law we'll discuss.

WORKBOOK

Chapter One Questions

Question: What people or circumstances have you allowed to control your life? What untruths have you subconsciously accepted by believing that you have no control over your own life?

_____
_____
_____
_____
_____
_____
_____
_____
_____

_____

_____

Question: List the areas over which you do have control (beginning with your own attitude) and those over which you do not (such as the law of the land, your past, news events, etc.). Are you spending more time and energy focusing on what you can change or what you can't?

_____

_____

_____

_____

_____

_____

_____

_____

Question: What are some things you can eliminate in your life? What are some areas in which you can delegate? Why do people feel they have to do everything themselves in order to be "in control" (for example, the control freak who won't allow anyone else to help)? How can eliminating and delegating increase your control over your life?

_____

_____

_____

_____

_____

_____

_____

_____

_____

_____

_____

Action: In order to take effective action, you will need to have clearly defined goals in place. Take a few moments to review your written goals. If you have never written down your goals, begin by writing down key areas (family, finances, career) and then listing two or three goals for each. With these goals in mind, evaluate how you can start living intentionally and how you can take control of each area of your life.

Chapter One Notes

CHAPTER TWO

The Law of Intelligent Practice

Outside of football season—in the spring and at summer football camp—we practiced running, jumping, and leaping all day long. But when the season started, our practice turned from developing discipline and getting in shape to a more intelligent kind of practice. We studied the past games and playbook of our next opposing team, and we tailored our practice so we would be prepared for that specific team. We practiced offensive plays that their defense was weak at stopping, and we practiced defensive plays based on their offensive play patterns.

My football team could have jumped and run and leapt like a herd of rabbits, but it didn't mean we were going to win any games. Contrary to popular belief, practice doesn't make perfect. We needed to transition from practice to *intelligent* practice.

A similar shift happened when I was on the police force. Every six months, we went to the shooting range to practice and to keep current on our required qualification to carry weapons. We practiced the conventional way: standing in a line, shooting stationary targets. Yet, what good would that do me on the street if I needed to use my firearm? In real life, the officer is moving—sprinting, ducking, lunging this way and that. The target is certainly moving, and there are almost always civilians in the mix, too, with everybody looking for cover.

So finally, one of our range instructors began putting us in real-life scenarios for target practice. Now we were running, ducking, laying down behind cover, and off balance, trying to avoid harming civilians as we aimed at fast-moving targets. We were learning street survival through intelligent practice.

As a child, I played some guitar. I never got very good, because I didn't practice much—or intelligently. But when I picked up the instrument again as an adult, I made significant progress. This wasn't because I practiced a long time, but because I practiced smart: ten minutes of scales, ten minutes of chords, ten minutes of strumming, and so on, until I'd practiced forty-five minutes. No dillydallying. My twenty-six-year-old instructor said, "I wish everybody would practice like you do."

This, then, is the second law: the *Law of Intelligent Practice*. It means we must practice with our goal in mind. Intelligent, here, means intentional and focused.

Do you want to win the football game? Then practice playing your opponent before you actually play them. Do you want to survive a street shoot-out as a police officer? Then target practice in realistic scenarios. Do you want to master a musical instrument or a specific skill? Then orient your practice toward mastery.

If you are going to succeed in achieving your goals, you need to follow the Law of Intelligent Practice. A slogan frequently used by early industrial engineers was "work smarter, not harder," and it has been applied to just about every field of work. This is the notion that hard work alone will not help you achieve your goals; you must incorporate smart work, too. And smart work includes smart practice.

Being intentional, focused, and goal-driven in practice is a biblical concept as well. Especially in the wisdom books, the Bible affirms the principle of working smarter, not harder. According to Ecclesiastes 10:10, "If the iron is blunt, and one does not sharpen the edge, he must use more strength, but wisdom helps one to succeed" (ESV). In other words, you can save yourself work by preparing intelligently before acting.

Now, I am assuming you're aware of the necessity of practice for achieving—well, anything worth achieving. Have you ever heard the phrase, "A goal without a plan is just a wish"? Unless you have a genie in a bottle, practice is a necessary component of accomplishing any goal.

Here are some points to consider as you pursue intelligent practice:

First, in your practice, *focus on your strengths more than your weaknesses*. An entire field of leadership and personal growth has been developed around this notion of soaring with your strengths and managing your weaknesses. A rabbit can swim when necessary, but it's made for jumping and running. Similarly, perhaps you can fumble your way around an Excel spreadsheet when necessary but you soar when you facilitate a team in the act of developing strategy. In that case, delegate spreadsheet work wherever you can and develop your strategic skills every chance you get.

Remember, the goal is to achieve the next level of success, experience, or mastery. If you spend your valuable practice time focusing on your weaknesses, you'll make only slight progress on them and none on your strengths. If you focus on your strengths, you'll improve overall. Don't practice for the sake of practice, and don't practice dwelling on your weakness. Practice *intelligently*. Intentionally. Intelligent practice makes the most of your day, whether you work 9 to 5, the midnight shift, or on your own schedule.

Second, *intelligent practice isn't really about an amount of time*. Are there some goals that can't be reached quickly? Sure. But none of them will come to fruition without intelligent practice. Plain old practice for the sake of checking a box won't do you any good. A piano student can't just put in a quota of hours playing scales, chords, and finger exercises and expect to shine at the recital—he or she must practice *music*.

Do you desire a marriage that's affirming and positive? Simply sitting next to your spouse on the couch won't get you there, will it? You must be intelligent about loving and respecting and believing the best of one another.

I am a product of parents who've been married more than fifty years. They didn't just say "I do," share the same address, and think everything would be hunky-dory. They *practiced*. My father practiced the daily, weekly, and yearly acts of kindness, love, provision, and encouragement that would bless my mother even after five decades together. My mother did the same. They didn't simply go through the required motions or pass the years. Instead, they intelligently focused on the goal—a lifetime of covenant love.

The fact that I've been married twenty-seven years and still feel like I'm dating my wife is testimony to the godly example of my parents. Their intelligent practice has further blessed the next two generations. I call that success.

Third, *practice is hard*. You know this if you've lived long enough to achieve anything, from playing with a Rubik's cube to making par on a hole to keeping a marriage in the positive zone. There's no getting around it. Intelligent practice is even harder, though more effective, because it requires intentional focus on a goal—you can't dilly-dally or just swipe a time card.

Practice is hard because there's no applause. We love to watch Kobe Bryant or Lebron James in the game, but we're not there to cheer at 2 p.m. on Tuesday when those guys are on their thousandth free-throw of the day. When I play those guitar chords and scales forty-five minutes a day, no one's there clapping for me. People might even leave the room to spare their ears!

Those long runs training for the marathon, those emails you draft fourteen times to get the wording just right, or the twentieth time you deny yourself a purchase so you can save money—no one applauds those small, daily, intentional, intelligent instances of you practicing toward your goal. It's hard to keep going, especially in an intentional way, without cheerleaders.

Practice is also hard because you're often doing it alone. Most marathon training happens on long, solo runs.

And nobody is up with you at 1:30 a.m. when you're finishing yet another paper for that master's degree. No one can achieve your goal but you. Success is about you rousing yourself before daylight. It's about you turning down the third cookie even when you're home alone. It's you choosing to do the right thing even when it's hard and it means you stand alone.

These days, practice is also difficult because we have so many distractions. Those extra appendages—also known as smart phones—are never truly off. Even if your ringer is down, that vibration notifying you of a text, email, or voicemail clamors for your immediate attention.

The ubiquitous nature of media is another contemporary distraction. Wherever you go, there are screens blaring news, music, sports, and endless advertisements. It's tough to compose music when you're surrounded by the songs of others. It's hard to read the business help book in the airport terminal when the news is always on overhead. And volumes have already been written on the fragmentation of concentration resulting from indiscriminate social media use.

There are other kinds of distractions we allow, too. We agree to things that aren't related to our goals, whether it's maintaining a relationship that is toxic, taking on house projects that will consume an inordinate amount of time and money, or doing volunteer activities that are outside of our gifts or skills.

Personally, I am spending less and less time doing a lot of things I was doing only a few years ago. I'm saying no more often so that my time can be maximized on the things that qualify as intelligent practice.

Intelligent practice requires a laser-like focus on the task at hand. Be ruthless at eliminating distractions. If I need two hours on a task, I focus on that task for the whole two hours.

The truth is, if you're looking for a reason not to practice today, you will find one. Practice is hard and often unenjoyable. We like what intelligent practice produces: the Kobe Bryant or the Jimmy Hendrix or the Warren Buffet. We like the calm persona, the disciplined calendar, the financial peace, and the meaningful career. But we would prefer to get to those levels of success overnight. We want to begin as a finished product—but that's simply not how it works. Not in anything.

Now, Apply This

Decide on a goal for your focus. Next, reverse engineer it. That is, work backward, step by step, from your goal, breaking it down into manageable increments. Then set aside a block of time each day to practice one of those steps. Do this *intentionally*. Use an egg timer if you need to, and for Pete's sake, remove the things that will distract you during this time!

Focus no more than twenty percent of your practice time on areas of weakness; focus at least eighty percent of your time on your strengths that will help you achieve your goal. Remember, you are in control and are responsible for achieving your goals. You'll need to practice intelligently to succeed.

That said, how can we practice intelligently if we're focused on the wrong thing? This is where the next law comes into play: mental equivalency.

WORKBOOK

Chapter Two Questions

Question: Give examples from your own life of the difference between practice and intelligent practice.

Question: What are your greatest hindrances to effective practice? Are you hindered by a lack of self discipline, a lack of motivation, particular distractions, etc.? What steps can you take to eliminate or minimize these obstacles?

_____
_____
_____
_____
_____
_____
_____
_____
_____
_____

Question: Are you wasting time focusing on your weaknesses instead of your strengths? How can you delegate areas of weakness and free up more time for areas of strength?

_____
_____
_____
_____

_____
_____
_____
_____
_____
_____
_____
_____

Action: Look back at your list of written goals from Chapter One. What sort of intelligent practice will be needed to fulfill each goal?

Then follow the steps at the end of this chapter to choose one goal and write out specific action steps for practicing it intelligently.

Chapter Two Notes

CHAPTER THREE

The Law of Mental Equivalency

You've probably seen this before: There was only one wreck, and it was on the side of the road. But the next thing you know, there are four other fender-benders within a quarter-mile. Why?

We call it rubber-necking. People are drawn to the blue lights, craning their heads curiously to see the cause, when *BAM!*—they hit the person in front of them. I saw it all the time as a police officer.

Why does this happen? Because our thoughts are powerful. What we think about, focus on, investigate, and dwell upon determines our course, just as drivers investigating the accident on the side of the road are more likely to get into accidents themselves.

Growing up playing sports, I had the story of *The Little Engine That Could* drilled into me.[5] Why? Because you have to believe something is achievable in order to achieve it. You have to *believe* you can catch that pass in order to catch it.

Before I continue, I need to issue one word of clarification about the *Law of Mental Equivalency*: it doesn't mean that "if you believe it, you can achieve it." Anyone who's lived long enough knows better than this. You might believe you can fly—but you really can't.

The Law of Mental Equivalency simply states that we will follow our thoughts. Our thoughts are powerful and charged, and they will lead us. Consequently, it is our responsibility to point them in the right direction.

A Hebrew scripture says, "Be careful how you think; your life is shaped by your thoughts" (Proverbs 4:23 GNT). This is the Law of Mental Equivalency—that we are a product of our thinking. When our mind is right, focused on a goal and believing we can achieve it, we become a product of that focus and belief. We're not drifting toward things that won't advance our objectives.[6]

We assume this principle in some contexts already, don't we? This is why we tell young drivers: "Keep your eyes on the road!" What do we tell athletes? "Keep your eyes on the ball! Keep your eyes on the net! Keep your mind on the task at hand!"

What is it we're urging them to focus on? *The right thing*. And why? Because thoughts are enormously powerful. Thoughts are charged. It's how a person in prison can nonetheless be free. It's how the oppressed can nonetheless rise. It's how someone can live in the slums yet radiate joy and generosity. Thoughts that are focused on the right things are charged and can move you, transforming your life.

You must take ownership of your thought life, understanding that no life change is going to occur until your thoughts are pointed in the right direction.

What does this mean? It means getting rid of excuses. Getting rid of negative thought patterns. Getting rid of unrealistic expectations—especially the expectation that change, or success, will happen quickly or easily. My father used to say, "Listen, it took you a long time to get into this predicament that you're trying to get out of. Change isn't going to happen overnight."

I've seen this play out in real communities. Five generations will grow up in one house, living and dying without ever leaving the house—let alone their neighborhood, town, or city—because their thoughts never went beyond grandma's house, the local schools, and a job at the refinery.

But you can control what is in your head by what you feed it. We all know we exercise control over our bodies by what foods we put in them, right? The Law of Mental Equivalency simply applies the same concept to our minds: we are a product of what we think, as surely as we are a product of what we eat. *Your mentality is the gatekeeper of your progress.*

Since you control what you think by what you feed your mind, feed your mind nutritious things and avoid detrimental things. What music are you feeding your mind? What speakers or teachers? What television shows or movies are you feeding yourself? What, if anything, are you reading? Don't even get me started on the empty calories of social media, which so often are nothing more than platforms for addiction to the vicarious thrills of others' highlight reels, mudslinging, and diatribes.

You control these influences. *You* change the channels

to the ones that will build you up, encourage you, challenge you in positive ways, strengthen your will, and give you effective tools to meet your goals.

The Bible encourages us to think on the things that are true, honorable, just, pure, lovely, commendable, and excellent (Philippians 4:8 ESV). This is precisely how we need to train our minds to think. As difficult as it may be, I have to find good in everything that happens to me. Even if something horrible happens, it is beneficial to focus on, and find strength in, the hope I have in Christ.

While this may sound like an impossible task at times, training my mind to seek out the positive rather than dwell on the negative is tremendously powerful. Without negating terrible events or situations, I still have to find something in them that I can learn or that will strengthen me.

Now, Apply This

How do we channel and strengthen our thoughts in the right direction? Here are some suggestions:

Journaling is a great way to keep your mind on the right things. Write down the direction you want your thoughts to go: the goals, reminders, and experiences you have that confirm and affirm your course. Occasionally review what you wrote to see your progress in the last week, month, or year, and to remind you of your direction.

Have *self-affirmations* available for review on a frequent basis. I have a daily alarm that goes off on my phone, and it's my voice saying to me, "Every day in every way, I'm getting better and better."

Draft a *personal mission statement* and review it daily. Mine is three minutes long, a reading I listen to every day. No matter who tells me what, I know who I am and where I am going. No matter what happens, that statement helps ensure I stay the course.

Eliminate the things you're feeding your mind that cause you to think in a negative or counterproductive way. Stay away from that music, that show, that website, that movie, that teacher, or those "friends."

Conversely, *pay attention* to the things you're feeding your mind that are wholesome and lift you up. Make a plan to feed yourself more of those: that music, entertainment, teaching, reading, or relationship.

Life is so sweet when you follow this law. You feed your mind wholesome food. You point your thoughts in a positive, powerful, charged direction. All of your life falls into line in sweet, positive ways. When things go south, your mental direction points you to your true north.

However, even when your mind is pointed at the right things, you need to have an expectation that you will get where you're headed. This need for the right expectation will bring us to our next law.

WORKBOOK

Chapter Three Questions

Question: Describe your most common thought patterns about your life—past, present, and future. Would you say these are positive or negative? Constructive or destructive?

_____

_____

_____

_____

_____

_____

_____

_____

Question: Do you expect change and success to happen quickly in your life? How can the right thought patterns enable you to stay focused and motivated when your efforts toward success do not yield quick results?

_____
_____
_____
_____
_____
_____
_____
_____
_____
_____
_____

Question: List the top ten influences on your thought life. Evaluate the extent to which each influence is pushing you positively toward truth, success, and goodness—or is detrimental to achieving your personal goals.

_____
_____
_____
_____

_____

_____

_____

_____

_____

_____

_____

Action: Looking back at your list of goals from Chapter One, begin to identify common themes. Use these themes to draft your personal mission statement. Remember, this is your *true north* statement to keep you focused on who you are and where you are going.

Chapter Three Notes

CHAPTER FOUR

The Law of Expectation

Have you ever heard of Tiffany Haddish? She's an actor who won an Emmy for her appearance on *Saturday Night Live*. She's also won thirteen other acting awards and has been nominated for an additional twelve.[7]

If you scroll through her Instagram account, however, you may notice she posted a photo from 2014 holding a friend's Emmy in her hand. She said that when she held it, she knew, "I am going to get one of these"—before she ever won one![8] It was just a matter of time before her talent and hard work earned her this coveted television award.

She had the expectation to power her drive. It wasn't pride or arrogance or any sense of entitlement; it was expectation that her hard work and perseverance would pay off with reward.

In this, Haddish personifies the *Law of Expectation*: whatever you expect with confidence becomes your own self-fulfilling prophecy. The related Law of Mental

Equivalency states that what you focus on, you will follow. The Law of Expectation states that what you *expect* will determine what you achieve.[9] You need both.

Successful men and women have an attitude of confident, positive expectancy. They expect to reach their objective. They expect to win. They expect to progress, moving forward and upward. The Bible encourages the faithful to have such an expectant attitude because they are firmly planted in a secure future: "And we know that for those who love God all things work together for good, for those who are called according to his purpose" (Romans 8:28 ESV).

When you believe in the future with that kind of certainty, your actions and behaviors will follow your belief in a determined, persistent way.

Therefore, we must set our expectations high. Having consistent, confident, positive, high expectations will bring multiple benefits. First, when we encounter failure—when, not if—we will expect to learn something from it. Our expectation of success will cause us to view our failures in a different light—as assets on the road to achievement. This is how successful entrepreneurs, star athletes, accomplished artists of all stripes, and excellent parents view setbacks. Thomas Edison is often quoted as saying, regarding his initial failed attempts at electric light, "I have not failed. I've just found ten thousand ways that won't work."[10]

Second, high expectations keep you moving when you're tempted to throw in the towel. I wasn't a great student. I failed tests. Some people would have given up, but I had extra patience to keep taking the test until I passed it. I came back again and again. Why? I had a high expectation of myself, and it wouldn't let me quit. When negative people came around or negative events happened to me, my expectation of eventual success propelled me forward.

How might your life change as you respond to what happens with a positive expectation? I encourage you to demonstrate persistence in the face of challenges, with your positive expectations strengthening you even in the midst of setbacks.

Third, high expectations are contagious. Once we start having them of ourselves, we're more likely to inspire those around us to set higher expectations in positive ways, with positive results.

For example, a buddy of mine is a principal at a school in a struggling neighborhood full of low-income ethnic minorities. It was a school without much hope; everybody expected the students to do poorly in all their testing, which proved a self-fulfilling prophecy. But my friend took over with high expectations for his teachers, his staff, and himself—and the students ended up scoring the highest in their district in their state's standardized testing. Dr. Drew's high expectations of himself led to conducting himself in a way that encouraged and empowered those around him who were already hungry to succeed yet lacked direction.

Maintaining high expectations of others requires knowing they are capable of great things. When you put that kind of faith in others, it automatically draws out those who are longing to do *more*. Dr. Drew didn't just waltz into the teachers' lounge and tell the faculty he expected their students to pass those standardized tests at the end of the school year. No, he poured time, praise, correction, training, encouragement, belief, and more time into those teachers and staff. His high expectations were accompanied by empowerment.

Good coaches do the same with their winning teams. Good teachers do the same with their star students. Good parents do the same with their children—yes, even and especially their teenagers.

The Law of Expectation does *not* mean you walk around announcing what a winner you're going to be. Your high expectations are for *you*, to help *you* handle failure, setbacks, motivation, and direction. They're not for you to share in a cocky way with every person you meet. If you incorporate acts of service into your life, this temptation won't be so strong. Pour into others; help them develop their own attitude of expectation for their lives. Then, when you share your own high expectations for yourself, you won't be perceived as "full of yourself."

Also, the Law of Expectation is *not* the same as having high hopes. High hopes are too near to wishful thinking, which has no basis in reality. Expectations are grounded in action and motivation. You have to work—hard and smart and consistently—to realize them.

Now, Apply This

Applying the Law of Expectation to your life is similar to applying the Law of Mental Equivalency. It's primarily about what and whom you allow to access your mind and your life. As with all of the other laws, you have to be intentional about this. Here are some practical steps:

Evaluate the people in your life as either a plus or a minus to your expectation level. Usually, within ten minutes of a conversation, you will know if a person is going to add to your life or subtract from it. As much as possible, limit your time with those who are a "minus" to your expectation level because they undermine your expectations of yourself, whether intentionally or unintentionally. Increase your time with those who are a "plus"—who raise your expectations of yourself.

On a similar note, invest in the right mentors. Spend time with people who have high expectations of themselves. If you know some people like that in your own life, spend time with them. Seek them out. Buy them lunch and ask to pick their brains for an hour. Choose books, podcasts, TED talks, and other resources from people or organizations with high expectations.

Analyze what you allow to influence you. Evaluate what you read, listen to, or watch. Which influences are teaching you important truths? Which are enjoyable? And which are you letting into your life without any real deliberation? Part of living with confident, positive expectations is consciously surrounding yourself with positivity.

You can't control everything that happens to you, but you must control what you can. You must focus your thoughts on the right things. You must have high, positive expectations of yourself.

But don't think it's all about you, all the time. The universal laws are also about how we relate to one another. Achieving our goals is never just about us; it includes blessing others. In the next chapter, therefore, we will explore the Law of Reciprocity.

WORKBOOK

Chapter Four Questions

Question: How would you define the difference between expectancy and egotism? Do you tend toward one over the other? Or, if you do not have high expectations for yourself and your future, why do you lack this confidence?

_____
_____
_____
_____
_____
_____
_____
_____
_____
_____

Question: Describe a time when a leader or mentor had high expectations for your behavior, performance, or abilities—or, conversely, one who expected you to fail. How did this person's expectations influence you? What lessons can you take from that experience to guide your interactions with the people under your leadership, now or in the future?

Question: *High hopes are too near to wishful thinking, which has no basis in reality. Expectations are grounded in action and motivation. You have to work—hard and smart and consistently—to realize them.* Are your dreams for your future based on high hopes (for example, winning the lottery or becoming an overnight viral sensation) or on expectations toward which you are actively working? Be specific in your answers.

_____

_____

_____

_____

_____

_____

_____

_____

_____

_____

_____

Action: List the qualities you are looking for in a mentor and identify a few people who could fill that role. Approach them with your request that they hold you accountable for pursuing your goals. If they are willing, create an intentional plan with them to keep track of your progress.

Chapter Four Notes

CHAPTER FIVE

The Law of Reciprocity

When I coached high school football, I made it a point to treat all of my players with the same belief, dignity, respect, and level of training, no matter their ability. But I also customized my coaching, and especially my mentoring of them, according to each player's strengths, weaknesses, needs, and potential. I didn't do this expecting to be repaid in any way. I expected nothing in return beyond the context of the football program.

But now, I am watching one of those players become a coach, and he's coaching with the same values and principles. I see him pouring into others without expectation of repayment. Did I ever get repaid for my pouring into this young man? Yes—he is blessing and leading the next generation with excellent values and principles. Watching my influence shape the next generation may not directly help me achieve my own goals, but it is decidedly a reward.

This is the fifth law we must incorporate and practice daily: the *Law of Reciprocity*.

Simply stated, the Law of Reciprocity is this: humans are driven to serve, and humans are driven to reciprocate one another in service. You will succeed to the extent that you serve.[11]

Let me quickly clarify what the Law of Reciprocity is *not*. It is not a "you scratch my back, I'll scratch yours" mentality. It is not a pyramid scheme like those employed in the business world. It is most definitely *not* the "Law of the Vending Machine," in which you put currency in and get a predictable, equivalent reward in return—it's not the relational version of $1 equals one candy bar. It can't be quantified or calculated, even though money or quantifiable resources may be involved.

The Law of Reciprocity is about outward focus: service, giving, being a blessing.

Like the other laws, this is based on a universal principle. Unlike some of the laws, though, this one is often countercultural. We live in a culture that is willing enough to give if the reward is immediate, or at least equivalent: "I do *x* for you, so you'll do *y* for me." We by no means live in a culture that encourages blessing for its own sake.

And let me tell you, blessing for its own sake *is plenty good enough*. When you bless others with your time, money, and talent, you will be blessed. The very act of serving another human carries enormous personal, communal, and cultural benefit. Your own sense of wellbeing is the minimum compensation you'll receive for your act of service.

But the Law of Reciprocity is more generous even than

that. When you serve, the blessing *will* come back to you in one way or another. Perhaps you'll mentor a young person who will then go on to mentor another in the next generation—and you'll see your work carry a legacy beyond you, impacting concentric circles of others.

Perhaps you'll be like my good friend Eric Brown, who owns JTP Transportation. His business was doing terribly, but he started intentionally giving his time, talent, and treasure to the vision of his church. Now his whole business has turned around and grown into a million-dollar transportation corporation.

Perhaps you'll be like my mentor Dennis Blackwell, who came to a dying church in southern New Jersey and led the members to give more. Now he's been serving and leading there for nearly three decades, and the congregation is flourishing.

Perhaps you'll be like the farmer who goes out, carrying seed to sow, and returns with sheaves of harvest (Psalm 126:6). You will reap what you sow (Galatians 6:7). If you sow generosity, gratitude, and service, you'll reap generosity, gratitude, and service. The key is to sow.

If we are going to achieve our goals and be successful, we must follow this law. Others will be willing to help us as we are willing to help them. If we want love or respect from others, we must give it first.

We teach this to our children, don't we? We repeat the Golden Rule to them, even if we ourselves follow it sporadically: "Treat others the same way you want them to treat you" (Luke 6:31 NASB).

Whatever you are lacking, start sowing it. Are you lacking financial success? Sow generously with what you already have. Are you lacking a meaningful support network? Sow into relationships with time and heart. Are you lacking opportunity? Sow into providing what you can for others. We give out of what we have, not out of what we don't have. We give out of our finances, time, talent and skills, knowledge, and connections.

Again, this isn't a vending machine. Don't donate to your church or your favorite cause and expect to get the equivalent financial payback in a certain way or certain amount of time—or at all. But if you pay attention, you'll notice blessing returning to you in some way or another.

Perhaps your car will last longer than expected before it needs another repair. Perhaps someone will donate a new appliance to you. Perhaps your performance review will go better than expected and you'll get a raise. Perhaps your bills will increase but you will encounter an opportunity for work on the side to compensate.

You will receive because you gave. That's how the Law of Reciprocity works.

God sends blessing to you, but He also sends blessings through you. The money I receive from selling this book will be sent out to others, because as long as it's going out and blessing people, it's changing lives. It meets my needs, but it also goes out and meets the needs of others. What do you do when your cup runs over? You get another cup and share with somebody.

If you work in the service industry, you will likely always remain employed if you are rendering great service. When I was young, I shoveled the snow for my neighbors, and they paid me better than the other kids—not because I was the only kid on the block shoveling snow or I shoveled snow faster, but because I offered faithful, smiling, over-the-top service.

We must rid ourselves of any self-serving mentality. The Law of Reciprocity will work, but only for those who adopt service and blessing as a lifestyle. It's not for those who give merely to receive or who only sometimes give selflessly.

There are, of course, obstacles to this mindset:

Ingratitude. Ungrateful folks simply are too consumed with all the things that are going wrong to be of service to others.

Dwelling on past hurts. This is similar to ingratitude but focused on past wrongs or grievances. Service is an act of living in the present. So long as we keep thinking about all the things that went wrong in the past, we're stuck there.

Unforgiveness. This is a doozy. Anne Lamott wrote this well-known quip: "Not forgiving someone is like drinking rat poison and expecting the rat to die."[12] The poison only hurts us. If we are harboring resentment or hatred of anyone else, it will be difficult to find a giving spirit within ourselves. This doesn't automatically mean trust or reconciliation with others, but it does mean you yourself have forgiven, for your own sake.

Negative or bad associations. Negative people will tell you that you're just being taken advantage of. They'll remind you that "no good deed goes unpunished," as the cynics put it. Minimize your exposure to such people.

Doubt. Doubt clouds your view of the blessing of being a blessing. Doubt whispers to you that helping others will make you weak or vulnerable; it maintains that life is a zero-sum game in which someone has to be a loser. Those are lies! Serving others makes you a winner.

Now, Apply This

To incorporate this essential Law of Reciprocity into your life, consider the following practical applications:

Be around other generous people. Watch how they give. Ask them how, where, and when they decide to give and what reciprocal benefits they've received. You need to hear success stories like the ones I've recounted in this chapter. Follow their example, in principle if not in specifics. Don't forget that we serve out of what we have, not out of what we don't have.

Be generous and remember that you're responsible and accountable only for your own behavior, not anyone else's. If a children's charity tells me their building needs a new roof and I give them a $3,000 check, but they end up using it to buy more equipment for the kids instead, that's okay. My responsibility is to sow the seed. God holds them accountable for what they do with it. Sometimes, I might be taken advantage of, but I will always be taken care of. When you are serving according to the Law of Reciprocity, no one can truly take advantage of you.

Follow the ten percent rule. Seek to give ten percent of your resources—time, talent, and treasure—to helping others. If you're not yet giving ten percent somewhere, build up to it.

Make a plan. Which of your resources (time, talent, or finances) do you have in excess? How could you give away ten percent of this resource? Is there a specific person or situation that needs it? Make a specific plan for your giving that also leaves room for spontaneous gifts when you see a need arise.

The Law of Reciprocity—like all seven laws, in fact—requires that we be habitual about it, not sporadic or halfhearted. And so, we encounter the next law: the Law of Habit.

WORKBOOK

Chapter Five Questions

Question: Reflecting on your life story, name the people who have selflessly invested in and influenced you. How does their service to you motivate you to serve others?

_____
_____
_____
_____
_____
_____
_____
_____
_____
_____
_____

Question: What are some intangible rewards that are more important to you than financial reward?

_____
_____
_____
_____
_____
_____
_____
_____
_____
_____

Question: What are some areas where your own "cup runs over," which could be opportunities for you to bless others? (These could be talents, skills, finances, large support networks, etc.) How, specifically, can you use your abundance to bless others?

_____
_____
_____
_____

_____

_____

_____

_____

_____

_____

_____

Action: Look back at your list of goals and your personal mission statement. Are they self-focused or others-focused? How can you adjust them to better reflect the Law of Reciprocity?

Chapter Five Notes

CHAPTER SIX

The Law of Habit

Here's the next universal law we must understand and follow in order to succeed: the *Law of Habit*. Simply stated, everything we do is a result of our habits,[13] which can function as stepping stones or as roadblocks—the choice is yours. Perhaps you've heard the true saying that first you form your habits, then your habits form you. That's why this law about good, goal-oriented habits is so crucial to master.

Like many people, I enjoyed reading as a child but found myself doing very little reading as an adult. Marrying and starting a family young, I couldn't get into the college or university I wanted to attend. Plus, I fell into the habit of always needing to please others. In practice, this meant that I hardly ever took the time to read.

But in my mid-thirties, I developed the habit of reading leadership books. This led me to seek successful people as mentors, which in turn led me to make significant changes in my own life—changes that resulted in a lot more success than I would have experienced if I'd continued in my non-reading, non-mentoring habits. I could have gotten into a habit like watching TV, drinking, obsessing over sports, or playing a ton of golf—but I didn't. Instead, I said to myself, *"Let me crack open these books and read. Let me take my mind to another level and develop myself so I can have a brighter tomorrow."*

We are bundles of habits that encompass the ways we walk, talk, act, and believe, the choices we make, the goals we pursue, and the people with whom we associate. It's cliché, but we humans really are creatures of habit. In short, habits are vitally important, because they shape us.

For this reason, the Bible emphasizes the importance of eliminating bad habits while establishing good habits that are in line with our goals, such as the habit of prayer. Psalm 55:17 says, "Evening and morning and at noon I utter my complaint and moan, and he hears my voice" (ESV). Daniel was in the habit of praying three times a day (Daniel 6:10 ESV), and Paul encouraged believers to "pray without ceasing" (1 Thessalonians 5:17 ESV). To maintain a close relationship with God the Father, Jesus habitually "would withdraw to desolate places and pray" (Luke 5:16 ESV) as well as pray with and for others (Luke 9:28 ESV; Matthew 19:13 ESV). The Bible encourages habits like praying, studying, and diligent work as powerful tools in our lives.

Now, there are four specifics you need to grasp about how the Law of Habit works.

First, understand that poor habits will develop automatically. They will grow like weeds—easily and rampantly. Bad habits will develop without you even trying. It's the universal truth of deterioration: left alone, unexamined and uncontrolled, everything in nature, from your backyard to your health to your life in general, tends toward deterioration.[14]

It's easy to fall into bad habits. We get lost in our careers. We behave just to please the boss, the spouse, the children, or the parents. We get lost in the grind of every day: paying bills, punching the clock, waiting for the vacation, doing the laundry and the dishes and the trash and the lawn, saving for the next car or Christmas or the kids' college fund. The days, weeks, months, and years pass by, without intentionality. We have to eat, and we have to pay the rent or mortgage, so we keep plugging away. We forget who we are and what our dreams are. We lose sight of who we're made to be.

It's easy to eat the cheesecake at 9 p.m., and it's easy to stay in bed another Saturday morning instead of going to the gym. It's easy to spend all that tax refund as soon as it arrives. It's no trouble at all to veg out another night in front of Netflix. Unfortunately, you don't have to make an effort to fall into negative habits.

Second—and this is obvious but needs to be addressed—we must get rid of the bad habits. The old Ralph Graves had a sweet tooth that was satisfied with a piece of cheesecake at 8 p.m. every night. Now I have just a little square of dark chocolate instead.

Do you want to lose weight? You have to lose the habit of eating what and when you want. Do you want to save for retirement? You have to drop the habit of spending above your means. Do you want to move up the career ladder? You have to drop the habit of bad-mouthing colleagues or bosses. And so on.

Once I stopped indulging in the cheesecake, I lost the weight. My bad habits were bringing about undesirable results. I had to honestly look at what I was doing wrong and change.

Change to what? Good habits.

So, third, bad habits have to be replaced with good ones. It's not enough to begin spending within your means. You also must make and follow a plan to save more—perhaps exponentially more.

We might have an old chair sitting in the house, and we put it in the garage because we're going to get a new one. But then we don't get a new one, so the next thing you know, the old chair's back in the house because we need a place to sit.

Likewise, if we don't replace the bad habit with a good habit, that bad habit will be back, probably with a vengeance. Just ask anyone who's tried to quit smoking without replacing the smoking habit with a good habit like a five-minute run, ten minutes with a good book, or a walk with the dog.

Fourth, your good habits need to be aligned with your goals. When I was on the police force, I had some good habits: I was always clean, my uniform impeccable. I arrived fifteen minutes before my shift. I stayed until the job was done, even if my shift was over. These were good habits! But they simply made me a good soldier; they didn't benefit my personal goals.

If your habits aren't leading you toward success, they're leading you toward failure. There's no treading water here. You must be highly intentional about your life and your life's rhythm. Your habits must be leading you toward your goals.

You might have a good habit of setting aside an extra five percent of your paycheck for an annual family vacation. But if you have a goal to take an extra vacation this year to celebrate an anniversary—or to take some days to visit colleges for your high school senior—you're going to need to increase the percentage you save. That's a new, very goal-focused habit to build.

The key is (a) to know your goal and (b) to reverse-engineer it in order to build goal-oriented habits.

For example, if your goal is to finish another degree, then sit down and work backward from your goal, setting sub-goals or steps that need to be achieved along the way and determining what habits you need to develop to achieve each of those steps.

Perhaps you need to change your weekday schedule to accommodate study time, so you give yourself a few weeks to adjust your schedule and get used to the new routine. Now you have a habit created and oriented toward a specific goal. Perhaps you need to cut out the daily run to Starbucks so you can afford textbooks—that's another habit created and oriented toward a specific goal.

Now, Apply This

Here are some practical steps to forming good, goal-oriented habits:

Set progressive goals, as described above, but time-specific. Set an annual goal, then a monthly, then a weekly, and then a daily, all within a specific context.

Ask yourself each day: *"What one thing can I do today to make tomorrow a little better?"* Maybe it's loading the dishwasher tonight to avoid interrupting your morning flow tomorrow. Maybe it's setting out your gym clothes tonight for the morning. Maybe it's cancelling your happy hour with the guys after work so you can go on a date.

Follow the five-second rule advocated by author Mel Robbins: Act on a great idea within five seconds, before your brain—or your fears or doubts or network of naysayers—can talk you out of it.[15] So, if you have a good idea, do it now, before you can finish counting to five. You will be amazed at how productive your day can become when you follow this five-second rule.

The last several years on the job, I sat in a police car knowing that retirement was coming up but I'd not yet poured into the person God had made or called me to be. I began to realize my life wasn't going where I wanted it to go, and if I didn't change my habits, I wouldn't change my life. That's when I started reading, studying, seeking out successful people, and learning from their habits.

Of course, there were hurdles in my own heart that had to be overcome in order for these new good habits to move me forward. One significant challenge was the matter of unforgiveness—which the next law will address.

WORKBOOK

Chapter Six Questions

Question: Describe a time when you overcame a bad habit or instituted a good habit. What motivated you to make the change and to be consistent about it? How can you use that experience to help you change your habits moving forward?

_____
_____
_____
_____
_____
_____
_____
_____
_____

_____
_____

Question: List your habits when it comes to food, time, hygiene, chores, free time, your job, etc. Which of these are good habits, and which ones are bad? Remember that a good habit will move you closer to your goals.

_____
_____
_____
_____
_____
_____
_____
_____
_____
_____
_____
_____
_____
_____
_____
_____

Question: Looking at your bad habits listed above, how can you specifically replace each with a good habit?

_____
_____
_____
_____
_____
_____
_____
_____
_____
_____

Action: Now work backward as described in this chapter. Look at your list of goals and determine what new habits you need to begin *now* in order to reach those goals.

Chapter Six Notes

CHAPTER SEVEN

The Law of Forgiveness

Some of us have the challenge of forgiving an individual. My challenge is forgiving a *system*.

From kindergarten through seventh grade, I went to a private Christian school. I was one of four black students out of five hundred total students. Can you guess what I received, repeatedly, from the white students and teachers—ostensibly Christians—at my private school? I was the object of blatant and regular racism.

By students and faculty alike, I was called names, told I'd not amount to much, and consistently treated like a second-class citizen. They regarded me as good enough to be on the baseball team, but not much more.

When I went to public school beginning in eighth grade, I fully expected more of the same. But there, I received only love. No racism from either Christians or non-Christians.

What's a person to do with this? I could reject the Christian faith altogether and choose another faith—or no faith. Or I could simply reject, or at least disassociate from, white Christians.

I'll tell you this: whatever choice I might make, there would come a point when I would have to forgive that system of white Christian racism. Why? Because so long as I was holding my grudges and resentments and angers, that system would control me.

I chose to forgive. It's an ongoing process, but it is absolutely and completely worth it.

This is the *Law of Forgiveness*: our minds will be healthy only to the degree that we can forgive others' offenses against us.

Friend, all seven laws are necessary for a successful life. If you master the other six, yet neglect this one, you will be hampered all your days—because forgiveness is that crucial.

Forgiveness lies at the heart of what the Bible teaches: because of Jesus' death on the cross to redeem those who repent, God forgives sinners who turn to Him seeking forgiveness. According to 1 John 1:9, "If we confess our sins, [God] is faithful and just to forgive us our sins and to cleanse us from all unrighteousness" (ESV). Believers are then called to forgive others as they have been forgiven, which is why the Lord's Prayer includes the words "and forgive us our debts, as we also have forgiven our debtors" (Matthew 6:12 ESV). If we refuse to forgive, we ultimately hurt ourselves—in part because we become consumed by bitterness.

Author John Bevere says that offense is the great bait of Satan,[16] and I have found this to be consistently true. When someone offends us, it's like bait dangling on a hook. If we take the bait, we're caught on that hook of offense and unforgiveness. When we forgive, however, we free ourselves from the hook.

Forgiveness is the most liberating act of life. By contrast, failure to demonstrate it gives control of your life to those you've judged to have wronged you. It's like in a story I often heard as a child, in which a snake crawled into the tool shed, cut himself on the hand saw lying on the bench, and was so "offended" that he attacked the saw. He bit it and cut his mouth, then wrapped himself around it—and, of course, died. Anger and unforgiveness will have a similar effect on us, mentally and spiritually if not physically.

In my case, while I didn't walk away from the Christian faith, I did distance myself from my white brothers and sisters. Because I was carrying my own hurt, I abstained from reconciliation and unification within the corporate church. My attitude was: "I'll see ya in heaven. I'm not part of repairing anything down here."

But I've learned I'll never be the pastor or the person God made me to be so long as I hold a grudge, even one against a system instead of a specific individual. I pastor in southern New Jersey—in a town known for its racism. Yet God has called me to have a multicultural congregation, which testifies that the Kingdom of God transcends the boundaries of race. I couldn't lead such a church if I were to harbor resentment against white brothers and sisters. That's how the Law of Forgiveness operates.

Forgiveness is an action verb. It is a decision *you* make: to recognize the wrong, to sort through the consequences of the wrong, and to forgive the offender so he or she (or it) no longer has control over your mind, spirit, attitude, or life course.

Because forgiveness is so often misunderstood, let me explain a few things that forgiveness is *not*. First, *forgiveness is not denial*. Some of us have had horrendous things done to us or to those we love. Forgiveness doesn't mean saying those things didn't happen, that they weren't harmful, or that they were too long ago to matter anymore. There's no statute of limitations on truth, and truth is required if we're going to walk in real freedom. You *must* be honest about the offenses and their consequences.

Second, *forgiveness doesn't necessarily lead to reconciliation*, although it can. Often, the offender doesn't realize he or she hurt you. Calm communication may elicit a sincere apology, and you can both move forward to reconciliation. But unfortunately, this doesn't always happen. Sometimes the offender is dead. Sometimes you don't even know where the person is, so you can't communicate. And sometimes the offender simply refuses to change. A wife may forgive an adulterous husband, but if he walks out on her for good, she can't force reconciliation. Forgiveness takes only one; reconciliation takes two.

Third, *forgiveness doesn't equal trust*, either. You may forgive someone, and your relationship may even be reconciled, but you don't necessarily have to trust them. Forgiveness is a gift, while trust is earned. With the wife and husband described above, the wife may offer the gift of forgiveness, and the two may be reconciled, but it will take *time* for trust to be restored.

After all, if a man hits me over the head with a backpack, I'll forgive him, but I won't keep walking down the hall where he's waiting to hit me again.

Fourth, *forgiveness is almost never instant.* It's a process. Depending on the hurt, it may require therapy, counseling, or a recovery program. All of these may be good and helpful things, and they should be pursued wholeheartedly as needed. Furthermore, even once you've forgiven someone—or as in my case, a system—you will likely have to remind yourself of the fact. Just as a one-time massage for a severe kink in your neck isn't sufficient, and you'll have to go back to the massage therapist, you will likely have to keep "massaging" your mind to remind yourself you've forgiven.

Fifth, *forgiveness is not freedom from consequence.* I can forgive my five-year-old for breaking Grandmama's cookie jar, but he's still going to have to clean up the mess, apologize, and offer to replace it. More seriously, you can forgive your abuser—but he or she still needs to pay the consequences of the sin and wrong committed.

Unforgiveness hinders creativity. It limits your growth. It limits your ideas. It keeps you bound to your offender and under his or her control, whether the other person is aware of it or not. Forgiveness gets you off that hook and frees you from that hold.

Moreover, forgiveness is crucial to your success. When you forgive, you have space in your mind and in your heart to breathe, be creative, move forward, and access all of your emotions in a healthy way.

Now, Apply This

I realize this just might be the toughest of the seven

universal laws to put into practice, but it is a linchpin and a foundation for holding up all the others. You might not read about it in all of the other "how to succeed" books, but I promise you it's crucial to any pursuit of success in your life.

A few practical ideas:

Whenever possible, communicate with the person you feel has wronged you. Minor offenses, in particular, are often unintentional. If you want healthy relationships, do all you can to keep the air clear between you and another. These conversations aren't easy, and there are no guarantees, but particularly among friends or reasonable colleagues, often the offender is as keen as you are to keep your relationship smooth. Give it a chance.

Write down the things that have hurt you. This might be in a journal. It might be in a letter addressed to that very person—you don't ever have to mail it or email it, but it will help you to have written it. You cannot forgive the wrongs you're keeping locked up and shut up inside of you. To deal with those hurts, you have to access them, first.

Write out your forgiveness. Again, you may or may not send that letter or email to the offender, but the act of translating your forgiveness into the written word can itself be a powerful act of forgiveness. Or you could set an empty chair across from you and privately role-play your offer of forgiveness to the person.

If you have hurts that have been choking you for a long time, please seek excellent counsel. A trusted friend, a counselor, a therapist, a psychiatrist—we have these human resources for emotional and mental freedom. Avail yourself of them as much as you can. Doing so is a sign of strength and resolve, not of weakness.

With the Law of Forgiveness as your foundation, and the six other universal laws built into a magnificent arch over your life, you will find yourself well on your way to meeting your goals—and to becoming the person you were meant to be. You will be in the sweet spot that blesses you, your family, your friends, your community, and even your world.

You will be unstoppable.

WORKBOOK

Chapter Seven Questions

Question: Is there a person, group, or system toward which you are harboring unforgiveness? How, exactly, might your unforgiveness be holding you back from achieving your fullest potential?

_____

_____

_____

_____

_____

_____

_____

_____

_____

_____

_____

Question: Which misconception about forgiveness—what it is and is not—has hindered you from forgiving your offenders? How can a proper understanding of forgiveness put it within reach, even when the offense has been severe?

_____

_____

_____

_____

_____

_____

_____

_____

_____

Question: Who are your heroes? Can you think of a person—from history or your own life—who forgave a huge wrong done against him or her? How was this person able to forgive? How did forgiveness influence the course of the person's life and legacy?

Action: If unforgiveness is keeping you from reaching your full potential, read a book or listen to a message devoted to this topic. Depending on the depth of the hurt and the nature of the offense, seek out a counselor who can help you work through traumatic past events and guide you toward freedom and forgiveness.

Chapter Seven Notes

CONCLUSION

Life According to the Laws

A goal without a plan is just a wish.

I woke up one morning when I was in my thirties, looked around, and thought to myself, "Is this what I was made for? I'm going to retire, Lord willing, in another ten years or so. What will I do with myself then? Play golf for the next thirty years? What kind of legacy am I setting up for myself?"

Frankly, I had no good answers for myself, so I started digging into those questions more deeply. I started reading. I started intentionally observing successful people—some I knew, some I only knew of—and whenever I could, I sat down with them and picked their brains. Because of my Christian faith, I started spending chunks of time with God, seeking His ways and wisdom and guidance.

What I discovered—and I'd seen it plenty in my years on the police force—is that no matter their race, education level, gender, socioeconomic status, or personal history, there was one thing all successful people had in common:

a responsible, positive *mindset.* It all came down to the way they thought—how they took control and focused their thoughts on the right things, how they expected their lives to proceed, how they formed good habits, whether they were committed to acts of service, and how they forgave.

So I followed their excellent examples. In short, with God's help, I took charge. I initiated forgiveness. I served others for the sake of serving, trusting that my service would somehow be reciprocated. I set clear goals, established habits that would be stepping stones to them, and expected that I would succeed—though even when I failed, it would serve as a lesson for growth.

And it worked! God has blessed me with success in ways I could not have imagined even a decade ago, certainly not as a college dropout who had struggled to support his wife and infant daughter only a decade or so before that.

The laws I've presented in this book work. They work for everyone who applies them consistently. Within one to three years, they will change your life if you follow them. By contrast, failure to apply them is like going through life without a safety belt.

So many of us are accustomed to being down, broken, and overlooked. We've felt it in our spirits, health, attitude, and expectations. Some of us are so used to being miserable that we don't even notice how miserable we are anymore.

But none of us has to stay there. I am walking proof of this. We *can* succeed if we take the laws to heart and incorporate them into our lives, one at a time, until they become second nature.

When you get up in the morning and look in the mirror, tell yourself, "*I'm going to live with expectation. I'm going to be intentional. I'm going to change my life, starting today. It's up to me, and I have the power to make it happen. It's my responsibility, no one else's, and I can do it. I will live courageously from this day forward.*"

Here are the steps to incorporating these seven universal laws into your life:

1. Choose the law that you have the greatest chance of success at making an integral part of your life right now. Don't bite off the biggest piece. Early success will give you some momentum. None of the laws are easy to practice fully, but there's probably one law that you can look at and say, "Okay, I can do that one first."

2. Start it today. (Remember the five-second rule?) At the end of each chapter, I've given you some practical ideas for application, but there are many more—brainstorm! Seek the wisdom of God and of wise, successful people in your life, especially those who believe in you most.

3. Fight fear. Fight it with everything you have! It takes tremendous courage to live intentionally; everything in our culture will resist you on this. And it takes tremendous courage to change, because fear will resist you at every turn: fear of failure, fear of change, fear of rejection. Put that fear aside and *jump* into becoming the person you

were made to be.

4. Write things down. Write down your fears. Write down your goals and the steps you need to achieve them. Write down the lessons you learn from your failures—that's how failure serves success! Write down your successes, too. Then review what you've written.

5. Interact with people who will encourage you, challenge you, inspire you, and support you with prayer, time, or resources.

6. As far as possible, eliminate—or at least, minimize—the time you spend around people who are "minuses," including those who remind you of your failures or your hurts. Those who hurt you, who are negative, who take and never give, or who draw you into careless living fall into this category. That said, some people will start out as "minuses" but become inspired by you and change along with you. Increasingly, those who don't will likely withdraw from you of their own accord, which is okay.

7. Celebrate your successes.

8. Pick another law to incorporate. Repeat steps 1–7.

Friend, you may have been the scaredy-cat lion in Oz up until now, but I promise you that if you begin to incorporate these laws, you will be infused with courage. You were made to make an impact! You were made to live for, and as part of, something bigger than yourself. These laws will help you get there—to a life that positively impacts others. This transformed life will change you and those around you for the better in the long term.

You will feel truly alive. And who knows where you'll land? Nobody expected me to be successful, but by following these universal principles, by the grace of God, I am successful today. Follow these seven laws and *you, too, will find success.*

REFERENCES

Notes

1. Tracy, Brian. "The Law of Control." *100 Absolutely Unbreakable Laws of Business Success.* Berrett-Koehler Publishers, 2002.

2. Tracy, Brian. *100 Absolutely Unbreakable Laws of Business Success.* Berrett-Koehler Publishers, 2002.

3. Schwantes, Marcel. "Warren Buffett Says This 1 Simple Habit Separates Successful People from Everyone Else." *Inc.com.* January 18. 2018. https://www.inc.com/marcel-schwantes/warren-buffett-says-this-is-1-simple-habit-that-separates-successful-people-from-everyone-else.html.

4. "One Change That Can Make All the Difference with Money." *Dave Ramsey Blog.* https://www.daveramsey.com/blog/one-change-makes-all-the-difference-with-money.

5. Piper, Watty. *The Little Engine That Could.* Platt & Munk, 1930.

6. Holmes, Ernest. *The Science of the Mind: The Definitive Edition.* Penguin, 1998.

7. "Tiffany Haddish." *IMDB.* https://www.imdb.com/name/nm1840504.

8. "@tiffanyhaddish." *Instagram.* https://www.instagram.com/p/BnpAk2YhrB1/?utm_source=ig_share_sheet&igshid=3h30bpsj9tyd.

9. Erickson, Milton. *My Voice Will Go with You."* W.W. Norton & Company, 1991.

10. Edison, Thomas. "How to Succeed as an Inventor." *The Christian Union.* June 15, 1882. N.Y. and Brooklyn Publishing Co., 1882, p. 544.

11. Kimbro, Dennis P. *What Makes the Great Great: Strategies for Extraordinary Achievements.* Broadway Books, 1998.

12. Lamott, Anne. *Traveling Mercies: Some Thoughts on Faith.* Anchor, 2000.

13. James, William. "The Law of Habit." February 1883. In *The Popular Science Monthly* 30, no. 4 (1887), D. Appleton & Company, p. 433.

14. Lucas, Jim. "What Is the Second Law of Thermodynamics." *Live Science.* May 22, 2015. https://www.livescience.com/50941-second-law-thermodynamics.html.

15. Robbins, Mel. *The 5 Second Rule.* Savio Republic, 2017.

16. Bevere, John. *The Bait of Satan: Living Free from the*

Deadly Trap of Offense. Charisma House, 1973.

APPENDIX

Recommended Reading

Authors and Speakers

John Bevere

E. M. Bounds

John Maxwell

Tony Robbins

Jim Rohn

Ronda Rousey

Brian Tracy

Zig Ziglar

Books

What Makes the Great Great? by Dennis Kimbro

The Four-Hour Workweek by Timothy Ferriss

Deep Work by Cal Newport

The 21 Irrefutable Laws of Leadership by John Maxwell

Extreme Ownership by Jocko Willink and Leif Babin

The Holy War by John Bunyan

The 5-Second Rule by Mel Robbins

The Charge by Brendon Burchard

Totally Fulfilled by Dean Graziosi

The One Thing by Gary Keller and Jay Papasan

The 15 Invaluable Laws of Growth by John Maxwell

About the Author

Ralph D. Graves Jr. serves as founder and senior pastor of Cornerstone Community Church in Millville, NJ. He is also a motivational speaker, business consultant, and author. Mr. Graves is the founder and vice president of City's Hope Community Development Corporation and founder of Project U. He is a member of the National Speakers Association (National and Philadelphia chapters). In 2011, he retired as a Sergeant of Police after twenty years of dedicated service to the State of New Jersey.

Having been certified by the John Maxwell Team as a coach, speaker, and leadership trainer, Mr. Graves decided to pair his newly acquired training with his business experience to create Project U: Executive Coaching & Leadership Multiplier. Project U offers customizable training programs, resources, and assessment tools that have proven capable of developing, improving, and multiplying leadership through the unique Cornerstone System.

Ralph Graves has succeeded in many endeavors, but nothing compares to his *greatest* accomplishment: being married to his high school sweetheart, his best friend, his wife—Christine Graves—for twenty-eight years. He and Christine have three children and three grandchildren.

About Speak It To Book

Speak It to Book, the premier ghostwriting agency and publisher for faith-filled thought leaders, is revolutionizing how books are created and used.

We are a team of world-changing people who are passionate about making your great ideas famous.

Imagine:

- What if you had a way to beat writer's block, overcome your busy schedule, and get all of those ideas out of your head?

- What if you could partner with a team to crush lack of motivation and productivity so you can get your story in front of the people who need it most?

- What if you took that next step into significance and influence, using your book to launch your platform?

- What if you could write your book with a team of professionals from start to finish?

Your ideas are meant for a wider audience. Visit www.speakittobook.com to schedule a call with our team of Jesus-loving publishing professionals today.

Made in the USA
Middletown, DE
13 August 2019